Art Smart

How to Draw Trucks and Cars

Christine Smith

For a free color catalog describing Gareth Stevens' list of high-quality books and multimedia programs, call 1-800-542-2595 (USA) or 1-800-461-9120 (Canada). Gareth Stevens Publishing's Fax: (414) 225-0377.

Library of Congress Cataloging-in-Publication Data

Smith, Christine (Christine Hunnikin)
How to draw trucks and cars / by Christine Smith.
p. cm. --(Art smart)
Includes index.
Summary: Step-by-step instructions for drawing several different types of trucks and cars.
ISBN 0-8368-1611-0 (library binding)
1. Trucks in art--Juvenile literature. 2. Automobiles in art--Juvenile literature. 3. Drawing--Technique--Juvenile literature.
[1. Trucks in art. 2. Automobiles in art. 3. Drawing--Technique.]
I. Title. II. Series.
NC825.T76S64   1996
743'.896292--dc20   95-53867

First published in North America in 1996 by
Gareth Stevens Publishing, 1555 North RiverCenter Drive, Suite 201, Milwaukee, Wisconsin, 53212, USA.
Original © 1993 by Regency House Publishing Limited (Troddy Books imprint), The Grange, Grange Yard, London, England, SE1 3AG. Text and illustrations by Christine Smith. Additional end matter © 1996 by Gareth Stevens, Inc.

Printed in the United States

4 5 6 7 8 9 99

Gareth Stevens Publishing
MILWAUKEE

Materials

Drawing pencils have letters printed on them to show the firmness of the lead. Pencils with an *H* have very hard lead. Pencils with an *HB* have medium lead. Pencils with a *B* have soft lead. Use an *HB* pencil to draw the outlines in this book. Then use a *B* pencil to complete the drawings.

This type of pencil sharpener works well because it keeps the shavings inside a container.

Once you have drawn the outlines on a piece of paper, place a thinner sheet of paper over them. Then make a clean, finished drawing, leaving out any unnecessary lines.

Use a soft eraser to make any changes you might want. Color your drawings with felt-tip pens, watercolors, crayons, or colored pencils.

Shapes

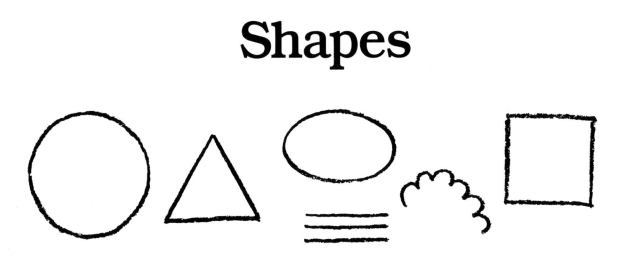

Before you begin drawing, practice the shapes above. Draw them over and over again. All the drawings in this book are based on these simple shapes.

Color

Mixing colors is fun whether you are using colored pencils or paints. Mix red and yellow to make orange. Mix blue and yellow to make green. Red and blue make purple.

A ruler and compass are useful tools for drawing trucks and cars.

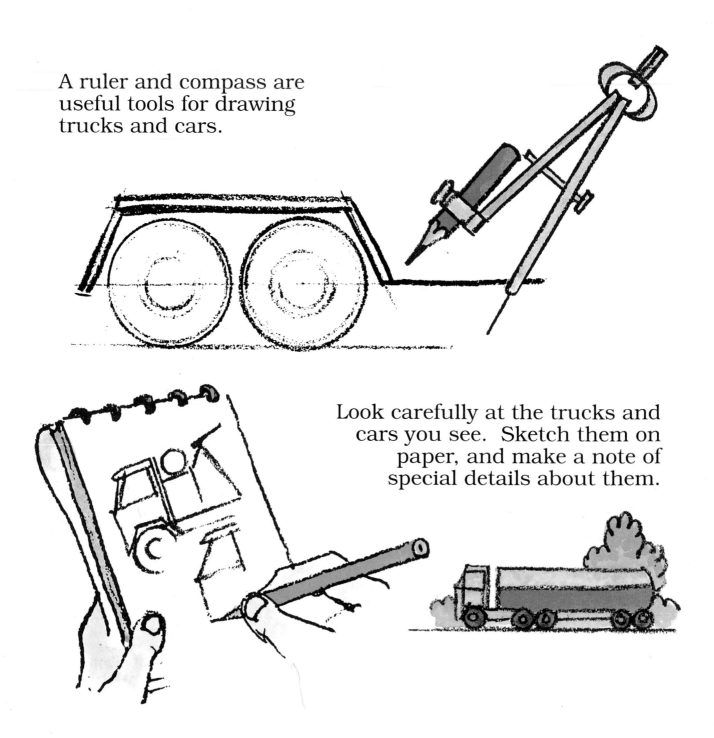

Look carefully at the trucks and cars you see. Sketch them on paper, and make a note of special details about them.

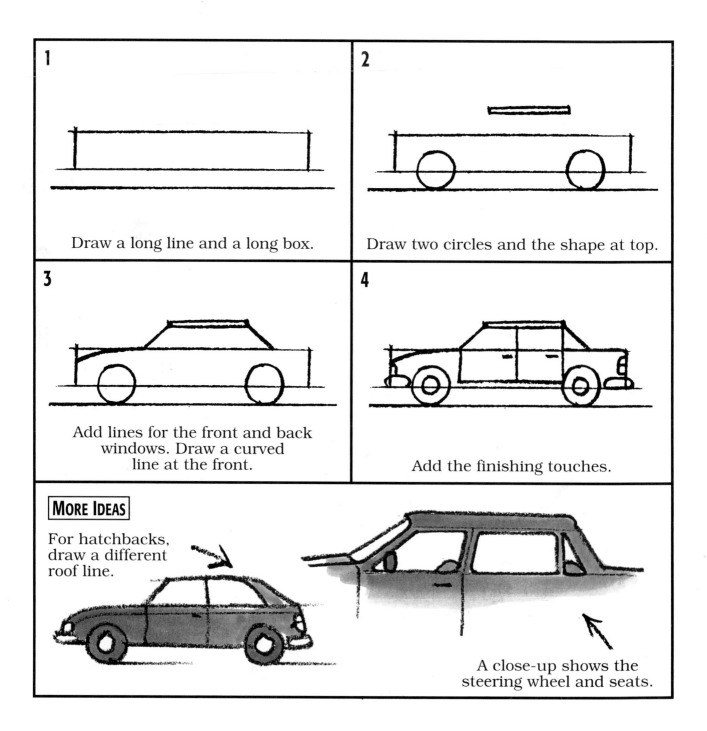

1
Draw a long line and a long box.

2
Draw two circles and the shape at top.

3
Add lines for the front and back windows. Draw a curved line at the front.

4
Add the finishing touches.

MORE IDEAS

For hatchbacks, draw a different roof line.

A close-up shows the steering wheel and seats.

Sedan

1 Draw a big circle and two smaller ones.

2 Draw in smaller circles for hubcaps. Add the frame.

3 Draw in the cab.

4 Next, draw the front . . .

5 then the back.

6 Add the finishing touches.

MORE IDEAS

Draw the truck emptying its load.

Draw rocks that are sharp and craggy, like this.

Dump truck

1

Draw a line and
a segment shape.

2

Add a center line
and a curve, like this.

3

Draw two circles
for the wheels.

4

Draw a roof
and windows . . .

5

more windows,
and a door.

6

Add the finishing touches.

MORE IDEAS

Close-ups of
the bumper
and lights.

You can also draw the
car as a convertible.

Volkswagen Beetle

1

Draw a bar and
two boxes, like this.

2

Add two circles
for the wheels.

3

Add these lines
for the rollbars.

4

Draw a seat
and steering wheel.

5

Draw mudguards
over the wheels.

6

Add the
finishing touches.

MORE IDEAS

Try drawing the
Jeep at an angle,
traveling over rough
areas of land.

Jeep

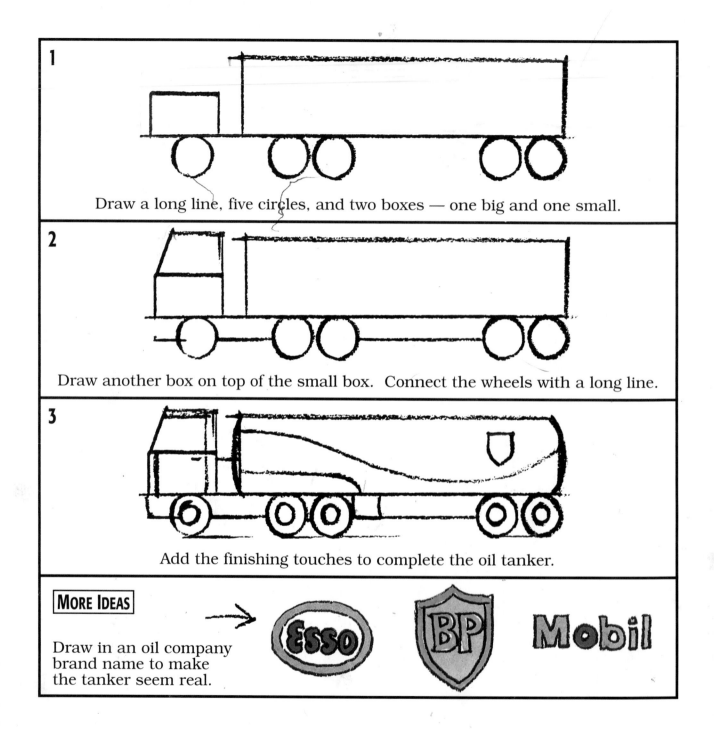

1

Draw a long line, five circles, and two boxes — one big and one small.

2

Draw another box on top of the small box. Connect the wheels with a long line.

3

Add the finishing touches to complete the oil tanker.

MORE IDEAS →

Draw in an oil company brand name to make the tanker seem real.

Esso   BP   Mobil

Oil tanker

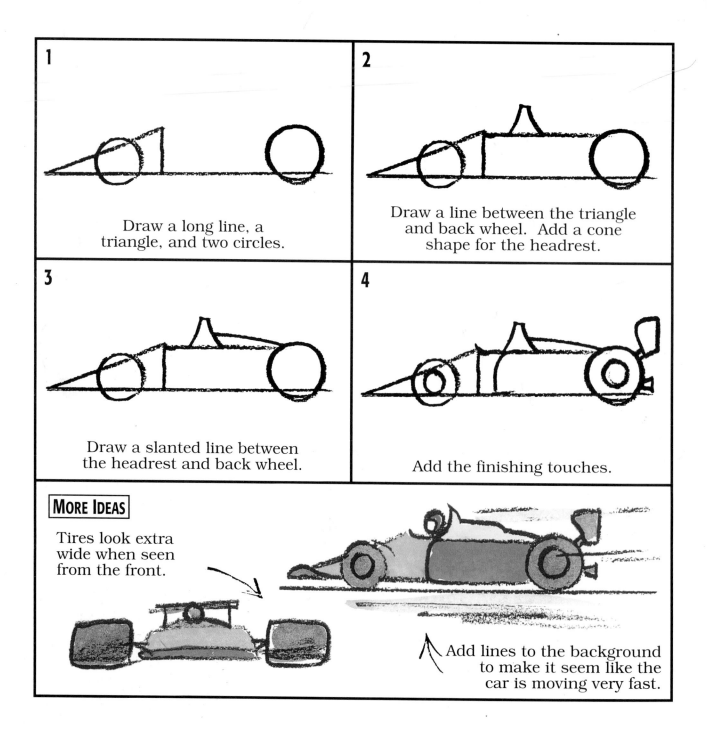

1

Draw a long line, a triangle, and two circles.

2

Draw a line between the triangle and back wheel. Add a cone shape for the headrest.

3

Draw a slanted line between the headrest and back wheel.

4

Add the finishing touches.

MORE IDEAS

Tires look extra wide when seen from the front.

Add lines to the background to make it seem like the car is moving very fast.

Race car

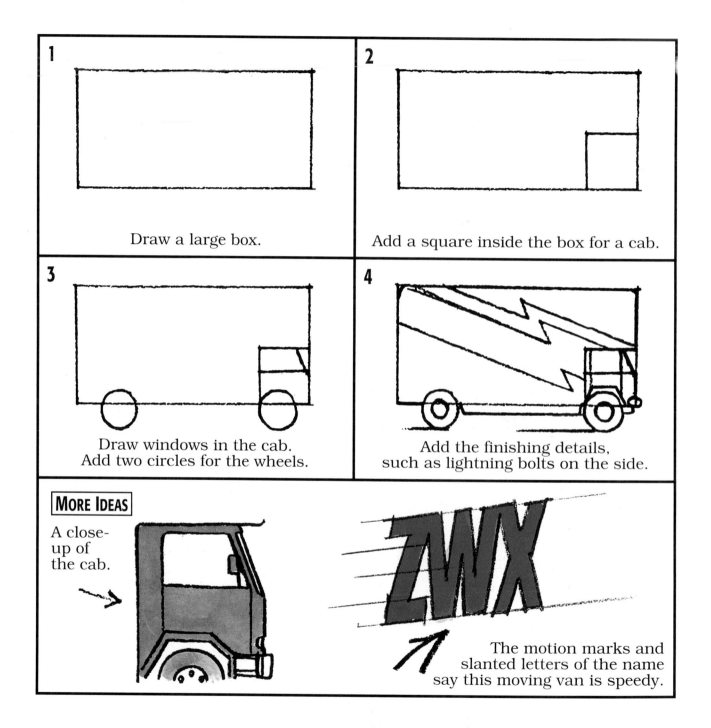

1

Draw a large box.

2

Add a square inside the box for a cab.

3

Draw windows in the cab.
Add two circles for the wheels.

4

Add the finishing details,
such as lightning bolts on the side.

MORE IDEAS

A close-up of the cab.

The motion marks and slanted letters of the name say this moving van is speedy.

Moving van

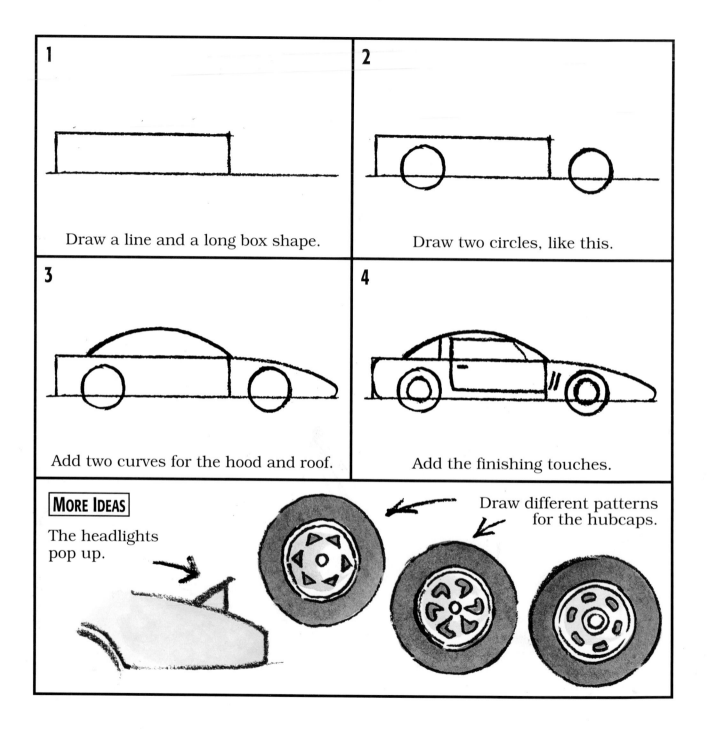

1

Draw a line and a long box shape.

2

Draw two circles, like this.

3

Add two curves for the hood and roof.

4

Add the finishing touches.

MORE IDEAS

The headlights pop up.

Draw different patterns for the hubcaps.

Sports car

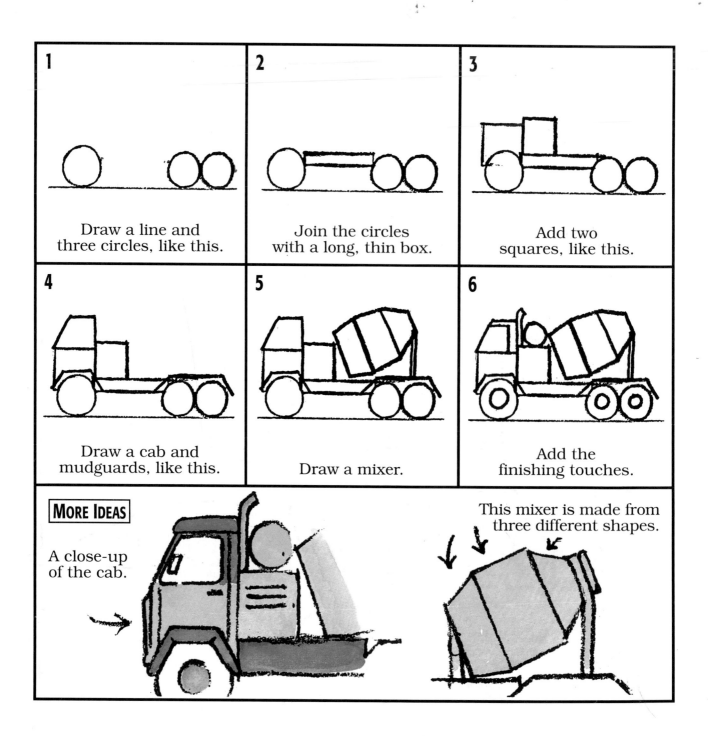

1
Draw a line and three circles, like this.

2
Join the circles with a long, thin box.

3
Add two squares, like this.

4
Draw a cab and mudguards, like this.

5
Draw a mixer.

6
Add the finishing touches.

MORE IDEAS

A close-up of the cab.

This mixer is made from three different shapes.

Cement mixer

More Books to Read

Amazing Cars. Trevor Lord (Knopf)
Big Rigs. Hope I. Marston (Cobblehill/Dutton)
Draw, Model, and Paint (series). (Gareth Stevens)
First Look at Cars. Daphne Butler (Gareth Stevens)
Four by Fours and Pickups. A. K. Donahue (Capstone Press)
Here Come the Monster Trucks. George Sullivan (Dutton Unicorn/Puffin)
How to Draw Cars and Trucks. Michael LaPlaca (Troll)
Make Way for Trucks. Gail Herman (Random)
The Picture World of Trucks. R. J. Stephen (Franklin Watts)
RVs and Vans. Stephen Burt (Capstone Press)
Worldwide Crafts (series). (Gareth Stevens)

Videos

Cars and Trucks. (Agency for Instructional Technology)
The First Cars. (Stories of America)
How a Car Is Built. (Think Media)
I Want to Be an Artist. (Crystal Productions)
So That's How They Build Cars. (Oak Leaf)
Trucks in Our Neighborhood: A First Film. (Phoenix/BFA Films and Video)
Trucks, Trains, and Boats. (Apollo Educational Video)
Wheels: The Joy of Cars. (Pacific Arts Video)

Index